Just So You Know

Just So You Know

Poems by

Edmund Conti

Kelsay Books

© 2018 Edmund Conti. All rights reserved. This material may not be reproduced in any form, published, reprinted, recorded, performed, broadcast, without the express written consent of Edmund Conti. All such actions are strictly prohibited by law.

Cover art: Edmund Conti
Cover design: Shay Culligan

ISBN: 978-1-947465-89-3

Kelsay Books
Aldrich Press
www.kelsaybooks.com

For Marilyn,

I never wrote you a love poem.
How about a book instead?

Acknowledgements

The following poems were previously published where noted:

Lucid Rhythms: "Just so You Know"
Abbey: "Death Warmed Over," "Fool Thou Art," "Godsend," and "Top Ten Reasons"
North Arizona Mandala: "Felicific Calculus"
Foundling: "Pain Comes in Two Sizes"
Barbaric Yawp: "Saint Frosty"
Plastic Tower: "People Like Us"
Light: "Un Bel Di," "Drake's Piece of Cake," "Look the Other Way," and "Raising My Spirits"
Orphic Lute: "In Memoriam," and "Bach to the Drawing Room"
Dog River Review: "Encouragement"
Studies in Contemporary Satire: "There Used to be a Title Here"
Soundzine: "But First a Few Lines"
The Quarterly: "Solace"
Negative Capability: "Badge of Honor"
Light Year, Bedford Intro. to Literature: "Pragmatist"
Journal of NJ Poets: "I(r)onic"
Bohemian Review: "Fall"
Folly: "Pied Pipers"

Contents

Just So You Know	11
The Hunter-Gatherer	12
Death Warmed Over	13
Felicific Calculus	14
Pain Comes in Two Sizes	15
Saint Frosty	16
Fool Thou Art	17
People Like Us	18
Un Bel Di	19
Haiku from Hell	20
Swan Song	21
In Memoriam	22
Encouragement	24
There Used to be a Title Here	25
But First a Few Lines from William Shakespeare*	26
Top Ten Reasons You're Going to Like this Poem	27
Bach to the Drawing Room	28
Solace	29
F-words	30
Badge of Honor	31
Drake's Piece of Cake	32
Look the Other Way	33
Two-Zone Heating	34
The Road Already Taken	35
Pragmatist	36
Godsend	37
I(r)onic	38
Sitting Pretty	39
Fall	40
Pied Pipers	41

About the Author

Just So You Know

I am not Billy Collins.
Just because we are both poets
does not mean I am Billy Collins.
There is no way I am Billy Collins.
For instance—cirrus, nimbus, stratocumulus.
Collins knows the names of clouds. He sees
galloping herds of albino bison or possibly,
just possibly, marshmallows fluffing.
All I see are horsies and duckies. And of course,
there is the matter of the Poet Laureateship.
Not that he lords it over me. I'll give His Lordship that.
Just a quiet unassuming guy. Like me.
He and his crate of mandarin oranges and
Russian novels. And me? Well, that's it.
If I have a ancient mourning vase from the Xin
Dynasty (and I do) it stays on the mantel
and not next to an album of Bix Beiderbecke
casually left out beside the half-finished
bowl of cornflakes and Belgium strawberries.
But that's Billy Collins. I'm not him.
And he's not me.

The Hunter-Gatherer

I hunt
through Poet's Market
and other listings
tracking down venues
for my poems.

I send them
to editors
who read them before
rejecting them. Or so
I gather.

Death Warmed Over

That's what my son said when I said
I wanted to be cremated. And, of course,
the other son, sibling that he is, asks
before or after you die? My wife
declines comment. She has already told me
she doesn't want any cameo appearances in
any of my poems. Unless it's a rhyming will.
No, she didn't say that. She could be very funny
if she would let me.

Felicific Calculus

I figured out
This happy fact—
I'm not devout
But still intact.

Pain Comes in Two Sizes

2 a.m. Time to try the right side.
The bed creaks. My wife stirs.
Maybe I'm better off on
my left side. Maybe I'm better off
dead. The refrigerator makes a new cube.
Life goes on. Back to the right side.
Clunk. Another ice cube.
Left side. What did I just take?
An Advil or an Aleve? Why do we need
so many ice cubes. Anyway, it's good
to have company. What a friend we have
in freezers. Clunk. Clunk Two cubes?
I'm being mocked by my appliances.
You have anything to say, Mr. Coffee?
You talking to me? Right side.
I wonder who else is lying sleepless
tonight. No I don't. I don't care.
Left side. No, no good. Right side.
Advil or Aleve? Pepsi or Coke?
One clunk or two? Time to count
to a thousand. Again. A thousand
sheep. A thousand cubes. A
thousand clowns. A thousand
points of light. Can it be dawn?
I sneak a look at the alarm clock.
2:06

Saint Frosty

It's cold and he hates it.
He doesn't know what else
there is. He has no racial
memory, no glacial memory,
of keeping warm. Warmth
is not in the snowman vocabulary.
In the snowman hagiography
Heaven and Hell are the same.
There he stands, freezing his balls off.
Or in this case, his carrot, trans-
formed from his head by the brat next door.
And thus he stands, waiting,
with a carrot for a banana.
Waiting to get warmer,
but he knows, somehow,
he knows, that it's not
going to happen and if it does,
it's not going to happen
the way he wants.

Fool Thou Art

What happens to the Fool in King Lear?
There he is in one act and gone in the next.
Shakespearean scholars worry about these matters.
These matters don't matter to the rest of us
who are wondering what happened to the money
we had in the last act. We don't make a scene.
We just cut back on the lattes and mall visits.
Ah, but those scholars continue to worry.
Maybe the fool is also playing Cordelia.
Note they are never seen together. Note also,
that I have never been seen with Billy Collins.
Nor have I ever been seen with my sons lately.
My wife says we should have never given them that money.
But we are not wandering the moors, I say,
This is only North Carolina. What about Edmund?
She asks. The bastard.

People Like Us

Some are.
Some don't.

Un Bel Di

Butterflies and moths remember their lives as caterpillars.
—Harper's

I well remember having all those feet.
I learned to walk at quite an early age.
Sometimes a friend was snatched (one weeps, one grieves)
But new ones would appear and, with them, love.

That's when I met the lissome furry Katie
And fantasized our legs all wrapped together.
Just one before the other; it was neat.
The trick was not to think; they would engage.

Oh life was lovely, lazy, eating leaves.
Avoiding, if one could, the birds above.
When I grew up I knew she'd be my matey,
Rubbing legs and more in caterpillar weather.

But she grew up to be a butterfly
And sad to tell you, readers, so did I.

Haiku from Hell

The barren landscape.
Do I hear the cry of the cicadas?
Hell no!

Cherry blossoms fall like the snow.
Are you looking for a snowball?
Look elsewhere, friend.

Cool, cool evening.
The blue heron flies across the moon.
We keep our memories

Cries of anguish.
Someone despairs even more than you.
Schadenfreude.

Are there birds here?
The call of the Bird of Paradise.
Listen to the mockingbird.

The optical illusion
That is fire and brimstone.
Thank God for sandals!

Cheer up, the red man says.
Things could be worse.
We all laugh.

Swan Song

I understand, I said, we mate for life.
She looked at me and paddled.
Then looked away and paddled on.
The lake was beautiful. Beautiful and calm.
No ripples from us. We paddled with the best of them.
A pair of old pros. Paddling together.
Clouds above us and clouds below us.
Does she dream of Zeus?

In Memoriam

John Betjeman cannot read his In Memoriam. Not today
    Or ever.

So what's the use of writing another jot.
    Why, pray,
    Endeavor?

For he who could best compose one is decomposing. Rot!
    Away
    Forever.

His spirit lives in every ingle-nook where England claims the heart
    And soul.

That poet so lightly musical, so serious and straight (an art)
    And droll.

Whose lines were seen and heard in every church, in every mart.
    And knoll.

Muckby-cum-Sparrowby cum Sphinx, Westmeath, Cheltenham;
    The set.

Henley-on-Thames, Highgate, Bristol, Clifton, Mint-on-Lamb:
    Gazette.

Places etched forever in his poems, each one a Betje-gram.
    Je bet!

We remember chintzy cheeriohs in his brilliant combinations.
    Cheeribye.

Farewell, so long, bunghosky, too—Goodbye to all his permutations.
    Never grim.
    Never dry.

Well, it's getting time for supper and we've had our ruminations.
    This is him.
    Dry your eye.

Encouragement

When we bent over the apparatus
The gym instructor would often pat us.

There Used to be a Title Here

I remember when Robert Rauchenberg
knocked on my door and said
he wanted to erase one of my poems.
Come in, I said.
I showed him this one. It wasn't going anywhere.
Editors had already told me that it was existential
in form but without any redeeming content.
(I'm paraphrasing, of course. Editors aren't that glib
or informative.) He looked at it.
Didn't read it. Just looked at it.
Looks good he said and took it.

Is there a moral here?
I hope not. Anyway, if there was one,
it's gone.

But First a Few Lines from William Shakespeare*

O, how I faint when I of you do write,
Not marble, nor the gilded monuments
Thus can my love excuse the slow offence
How can I then return in happy plight?

O, never say that I was false of heart
When forty winters shall besiege thy brow,
Thou art as tyrannous, so as thou art
Then hate me when thou wilt; if ever, now.

My glass shall not persuade me I am old,
Full many a glorious morning have I seen
That time of year thou mayst in me behold
How like a winter hath my absence been.

Weary with toil, I haste me to my bed,
No longer mourn for me when I am dead.

*Each line is a first line from one of Shakespeare's sonnets

Top Ten Reasons You're Going to Like this Poem

10. It has an interesting and possibly amusing title.

9. It will not mention Death Panels.

8. It has accessible irony in claiming not to mention Death Panels while cleverly mentioning them.

7. It will not use four-letters words for urination, defecation and fornication.

6. It will not poke fun at the less fortunate among us—welfare queens, half-breeds, people of previous turpitude, deathers, birthers, mooners, merry rhymesters and Republicans.

5. The astute reader will have a sense of when this poem will end.

4. It will provide the lazy critic with a witty rejoinder—"Top Ten Reasons Why I Hate This Poem."

3. The mounting suspense wondering what final reason could possibly top those already mentioned.

2. The happy realization that, despite the crate of blood oranges and the empty bottle of Peruvian brandy, this is not a Billy Collins poem.

1. And finally, the delight of the reader in knowing that he has been duped by the poet into re-reading this poem looking for those oranges and brandy (not to mention the pack of Camel filters).

Bach to the Drawing Room

Kings demandin'
Quick and dirty
Music. Branden-
Burg Concerti.

Solace

I know, I know it's tough.
I know. It's tough. I know.
It's tough. I know it's tough.
I know. I know. It's tough.
I know it's tough. I know.

It's tough.

I know.

F-words

Farting is funny.
Flatulence is not. Not
when it's yours. You're
constipated, one doctor tells me.
Go play some golf.
I need a second opinion but
not a second bill. The internet
has a lot of opinions, not
all of them contradictory.
I'm still searching.
More reports later.
Fore!

Badge of Honor

I have a badge.
It has my name on it.
It has my picture on it.
It tells me where I work.
I work in an important place.
I work in a government installation.
I am an important person.
When I go to work
    the guard looks at my badge
    he looks at me
    he waves me in.
I am an important person.
I know who I am.
I know where I work.
I know when I was born.
I know my sex and eye color.
I know my height in inches.
I know when I will expire.

Drake's Piece of Cake

The Spanish Armada?
De nada.

Look the Other Way

Any girl can be glamourous. All you have to do is stand still and look stupid.
—Hedy Lamarr

I was a stupid looking lad.
I had my curls.
I had my toys.
But glamour's what I never had.
It works for girls
But not for boys.

Two-Zone Heating

"Turn on the TV," he commanded
as he entered our house with his son.
It was too early for Oprah but who am I
to argue with a plumber. We watched
the first tower in flames and saw
the second take a hit. "The world
will never be the same." I said.
The plumber agreed and so
did his son. The men turned
their attention to our furnace
and thermostat. No major problems.
We were warm all winter.

The Road Already Taken

Poems that practice gimmickry
Aren't candidates for mimicry.

Lower case or funny punct.
Works for cummings but should be junked.

If you want to copy, copy freely
From poems considered touchy-feely.

Emulate the classic winners
Or Franoçis Villon and other sinners.

You'll find your feelings won't be lost
If you scan like Keats or Robert Frost.

If you want your poems to be as merry
As Ogden Nash, avoid Ashbery.

Short lines work for some. But who?
Kay Ryan, maybe. It's not for you.

Do you want your readers all to cry?
Take some hints from Robert Bly.

Or if you feel somewhat silly,
Check on Collins. You know, Billy.

Of course you can ignore the best
And just be liked. Like Edgar Guest.

Bad poems are made by fools like I.
So better find some other guy.

Pragmatist

Apocalypse soon
Coming our way
Ground zero at noon
Halve a nice day.

Godsend

Yesterday I got an e-mail from God.
Of course, I sent it to the spam file
wondering how it got through the filter.
DON'T DO THAT! This was accompanied
by what felt like a kick in the stomach,
a blinding light and roll of thunder.
So I didn't do it. NOW READ IT.
And I'm thinking, if we can communicate
like this why does He need e-mail?
DON'T THINK SO MUCH, POET, JUST READ IT.
So I read it. "Write a poem about Me."
And I'm thinking, nice touch, capitalizing
Me. Which got me another kick in the stomach.
I'm not a good poet, I said. I tend to write
light verse. And I could never do imagery.

WHAT! (Luckily no thunderclap.)
When I made the world I gave you
a lot to work with. Blue herons,
skipping stones, melodic tones, cellphones,
brown-gold leaf, sweet rice paper,
Beethoven, Gershwin. Ella.
Just write it all down, rhyme if you must.
No Moses jokes. And maybe put in a plug
for the Grand Canyon.
And I'm thinking, what I need is a Muse
not an Inspiration. (oof!)

I(r)onic

They
do
it
to
us
so
we
do
it
to
them

Sitting Pretty

The family-size box of cornflakes from Costco
sits on the front porch next to the refrigerator.
Too big to get through the front door.
The kids want it for their own clubhouse.
Let's eat the cornflakes first, I say.
Have to say they look kind of neat there,
all lined up—the ice box, the corn flakes and
the old green glider. There's a hole in the box,
halfway down, so you can reach in from the glider
and grab a handful of flakes. Jeb and Jim
like to come over, drink my beer and munch
on my cornflakes. Gliding and creaking
on the old rusty glider. Kicking at the birds
hoping for a breakfast of champions. No use
kicking at the squirrels. They are too fast,
the little buggers and besides, they keep
the porch floor clean. The mocking bird
declines our largess. Sits in the pin oak
mocking us. Sing to your heart's content,
little birdie, and then fly off and see
if you can round up some food.

Fall

Two leaves
One leaves
One leaf

Pied Pipers

Glory be to God for dabbling poets—
    For versifiers who like to try their hand
        And heart at some poetic gem:

A villanelle that strains to overflow its
    Limits. Sonnets, perhaps, that show command
        Of rhyme and prosody and apothegm.

All poets, then, published ones or not; —
    In Poetry, in Dog Days Review, and
        Self-published, too, if that's their stratagem.

Respected and rejected. All!—the lot.
        Praise them.

About the Author

Edmund Conti has had the usual 500 or so poems published in the usual places (assuming Poetry and The New Yorker are not the usual places). He started off writing light verse and stopped, not because he became world-weary, but editor-weary, editors who were quick to say "if it rhymes we don't want it." So Edmund reverted to free verse, free in his case being the freedom to rhyme when he chose to and scan when it pleased him.

Conti won the Willard Espy Prize for Light Verse in 2001 and can't seem to forget that. He is still spending the thousand dollars that came with it. He also won the more forgettable Ruby Muse prize ($15). He has recent acceptances from Light, Lighten-up Online, Asses of Parnassus, new verse news, Rotary Dial and Verse-Virtual. He also invented a word game, "Bananagrams" (anagrams to drive you bananas) that ran for a while in Word Ways and Games Magazine.

www.ingramcontent.com/pod-product-compliance
Lightning Source LLC
LaVergne TN
LVHW091321080426
835510LV00007B/600